BEDTIME MEDITATIONS FOR KIDS

BEDTIME MEDITATIONS FOR KIDS

QUICK, CALMING EXERCISES TO HELP KIDS GET TO SLEEP

Cory Cochiolo

MA, CHt

Illustrations by Katie Turner

ROCKRIDGE
PRESS

For all the hardworking parents, caregivers, and teachers who shape our world through meaningful connection with children.

Contents

Letter to Grownups

Hello, friend,

Welcome to the wonderful world of meditation and all of its magical possibilities. There are many different ways to meditate, such as sitting in silence, doing breathing exercises or visualization techniques, and even meditating while walking. Activities like painting can also put the mind into a meditative state. In this book, l share many forms of meditation to make your child's bedtime routine a pleasurable experience for all.

I have assembled 30 different ways for children to have fun and unwind; become more aware of thoughts, feelings, and the body; increase their focusing skills; and, most important, teach them how to deeply relax before bed. The magic I share with you in this book has not only changed my life, but it has also helped thousands of other families using the ideas I suggest on my YouTube channel, Corys ConsciousLiving.

All parents and caregivers can relate to a child who doesn't like to go to bed when they're told to, and trying to force them to sleep when they aren't tired can be even more of a challenge. Close your eyes and imagine all that struggle disappearing, and instead see the vision of a happy, calm, peaceful interaction with your child at bedtime. The fun meditation games, interactive stories, calming breathing exercises, and other therapeutic techniques in this book will help bring that vision to reality.

I encourage you to explore the meditation exercises along with your child. You never know—they might help you, too!

Cory Cochiolo, MA, CHt

1. High Five

MOOD-CHANGING EXERCISE #1

This exercise is designed to help you end the day on a positive note. It can make you feel good about yourself while encouraging good behavior, because you are getting rewarded with a high five from your parent or caregiver. It also gives them an opportunity to see how awesome you are.

1. Lie comfortably on your back in your bed.

2. Close your eyes.

3. Next, take a nice big, deep breath.

4. Ask yourself, "What was something I did today that was good?"

5. Here are some examples: You brushed your teeth; you cleaned up your room; you were kind to another person; you shared your toys; you told the truth about something.

6. Use the fingers on one of your hands to try to count up to five good acts you did.

7. Think of even the smallest things—they matter, too.

8. Make sure to get a high five on the other hand from your caregiver for each good act that you share with them.

2. Tree Time

This is a relaxing meditation that will help you feel safe and secure before you go to sleep.

1. Lie comfortably on your back and close your eyes.

2. Take a nice big, deep breath and imagine you are lying on a forest floor surrounded by big, tall trees.

3. Focus on your feet and imagine that they are starting to tingle and twitch.

4. Now, in your mind, stand up tall, just like the trees around you.

5. When you look at your feet, see that you have super-strong roots growing out of your toes.

6. Now your legs look like a tree trunk. Your arms, body, and head have turned into the branches and leaves of the tree you've become.

7. A big gust of wind blows through the forest, but you barely move, you are so strong and solid. You are rooted to the ground. You are safe and secure, like the other big, strong trees in the forest.

8. Fall asleep feeling connected to the forest and feeling secure, strong, and safe.

3. Tell-All Turtle

EXPRESS YOUR FEELINGS

This exercise is excellent when you feel sad or something is bothering you and you are finding it hard to talk about it. When you talk to your caregiver and they let you know that they love you no matter what is happening, it will make you feel comfortable enough to share with them more often. Let this exercise help you begin to share your feelings with them.

1. Lie comfortably on your back in bed for Tell-All Turtle time.

2. Pull the covers over your head like a turtle going into its shell.

3. You should feel snug and safe inside your shell, and it might feel more private for you in there.

4. This is your time to tell all and share. Remember that this is a safe space, and you are a snug turtle in your shell.

5. Your caregiver might ask, "What's on your mind?" to get you started.

6. If you want, you can ask your caregiver to Tell-All Turtle first by sharing a worry of their own. They can do this by putting their head inside their shirt or covering their face with a blanket.

7. Now share with them what's on your mind. Let it out so you can feel better and lighter.

8. It's nice when your caregiver says, "It's okay. I love you," especially after you share a worry with them, so try to remember to say the same thing to them after they share a worry with you.

4. Cloud-Jumping Game

FLOAT INTO SLEEP

This visualization meditation is wonderful and playful. It encourages you to use your imagination and get some yummy cuddles from your favorite animals up in the clouds.

1. Lie on your back in your bed. Have a good wiggle and giggle as you move around and shake out all the tension from your body. After all that, lie still in your favorite comfy position.

2. Close your eyes and take a nice deep breath. See if you can make your body feel really heavy and comfortable, just like it would feel if you'd been running and playing hard all day long.

3. Now imagine that your body is starting to float off the bed . . . and up into the sky, weightless.

4. Find yourself standing on a big white fluffy cloud. It's soft and spongy underneath your feet.

5. The sky is full of big white fluffy clouds that look like the one you are standing on, but when you look closer, you see that each cloud has a different animal standing on top of it. All these animals are your favorites.

6. You have super high-jumping powers up here in the sky. You can jump onto any cloud and hang out with whichever animal you want to.

7. Pick a cloud and jump onto it. Stay on this cloud and snuggle with the animal that's on it, or jump onto other clouds if you want to. This is your own special cloud-jumping game, so you get to decide where to go!

8. Fall asleep on your cloud. Sweet dreams . . .

5. Check-In Time

AN END-OF-THE-DAY EXERCISE

This exercise is going to help you learn how to feel all different kinds of emotions. Talking about your feelings and feeling okay to feel them will help make you happier. Remember that you are safe to feel what you are feeling, and that it is all good and normal. You are awesome no matter what.

1. Get tucked into bed and make sure you are comfy.

2. Ask yourself the following questions. I encourage you to make these questions a part of your bedtime routine every night.

   * What was the best part of my day?

   * What would I change about my day if I could?

   * Is there something I am grateful for today?

   * What emotions did I feel today?

3. You can say to yourself, "Do I feel sad, mad, happy, jealous, or nervous?" Or maybe you're feeling something else. This is a great way to notice when you are feeling certain emotions that feel heavy or uncomfortable so you can process them in a healthy way.

4. If it feels right for you, have a chat with your parent or caregiver about your day and see how much better you feel to get it all out.

5. Maybe you had a super day and all your emotions were good ones. Share those, too!

6. This might get your caregiver to share some of the feelings they felt today, as well.

7. When you are finished sharing, say good night to your caregiver.

8. Go to sleep feeling good about describing how you felt today.

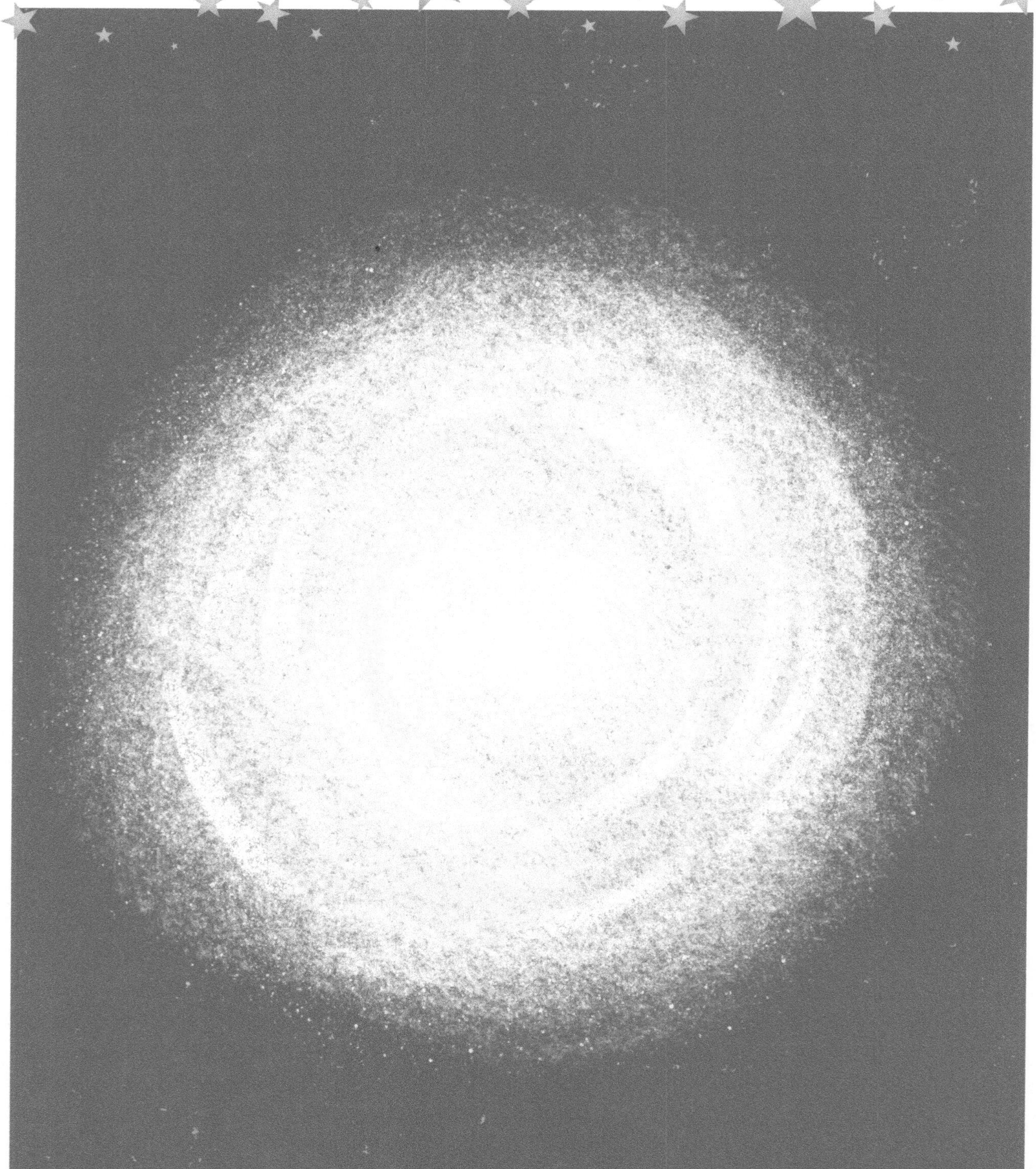

6. Vacuum Cleaner Breathing

This is a great visualization meditation for people of any age. It's very effective for changing a bad mood into a good mood, which is a perfect thing to do just before bed.

1. Make sure you're comfortable in bed.

2. Close your eyes and relax. Try to lie as still as a statue.

3. Focus on your breathing: breathing in . . . and breathing out.

4. Imagine there is a big white ball of light in front of your face. It can look like a huge white cloud or like the sun in the sky.

5. Now take a deep breath in and imagine you are breathing in the white light. The white light goes down into your tummy, and down into your arms and legs. The light fills your head and keeps going into you with every breath until your whole body is filled with this energetic white light.

6. This white light is like a vacuum cleaner. It cleans out all your worries and bad moods. If you are angry or sad, it will clean those negative feelings out.

7. Now imagine that when you breathe out, you see a big gray cloud of dust. Inside that gray cloud are all the bad thoughts and feelings the vacuum cleaner has sucked away for you.

8. Keep breathing in the big white light and breathing out the gray cloud that's holding all your bad thoughts, until you feel clean inside and you can fall asleep easily.

7. Bits and Pieces of Me

AWARENESS MEDITATION

This exercise will help you understand and love all the different parts of yourself. Sit down at bedtime and create fun names for the different pieces that make up your personality. For example, you can give one of your qualities a name like Lily Lovebug or Leo Lovebug—whatever name fits you. Lily Lovebug loves snuggles and kisses because they always make her feel better before bed. Silly Sam is funny, and he needs to be tickled or to jump around a bit before bed. Talking Tina (or Talking Tom) likes to chat about their day before bed. You can make up as many characters as you choose that fit your personality. You will have 10 minutes to chat about whatever you want with your parent or caregiver, but when that time is up, it's time for bed.

1. Get snuggled up in bed.

2. Think about how you feel tonight.

3. What kind of mood are you in?

4. Which character do you feel like?

5. Out of all the fun characters you have already named, tell your caregiver which character you are feeling like right now.

6. Have fun—cuddle, chat, and dance in that character.

7. Do whatever you want for the next 10 minutes with your parent.

8. When the time is up, it's time for bed, sleepyhead.

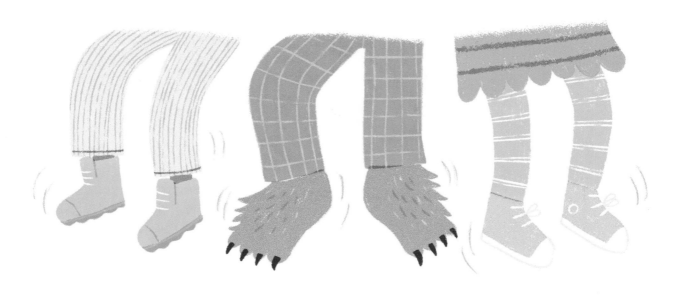

8. Monster Stomp

FUN EXERCISE FOR MANAGING ANGER

The idea behind Monster Stomp is for you to have a chance to stomp out your feelings. You will stomp your feet for each word in your sentence. The guidelines are to use "I feel" statements. For example: "I" (STOMP) "feel" (STOMP) "angry" (STOMP). Or you can say, "I feel frustrated because . . ." or "I feel worried because . . ." and then STOMP, STOMP, STOMP! The physical act of stomping allows you to release your built-up energy, like hitting a pillow or running really fast. Releasing the energy in an expressive way also helps you feel listened to, which is an important part of the process. Afterward, you'll feel better!

1. Think about how you are feeling.

2. In this moment, are you mad, sad, frustrated, confused, hurt, or lonely? How do you feel right now?

3. Now stomp out those feelings.

4. With every word you say out loud, stomp your feet at the same time. You can stomp while standing in one spot or as you walk around your room.

5. Stomp and express how you are feeling until you get out all your negative feelings.

6. Stomp until you feel tired or all emptied out.

7. When you are finished, you should feel satisfied and relieved of everything that was bothering you.

8. Now you will be able to fall asleep easily.

9. squeezing peas

This is a fun exercise to help you relax all your muscles before bed. Who doesn't want to squeeze millions of peas? I know I do!

1. Make sure you are comfy in your bed.

2. Lie on your back in a star shape with your arms and legs stretched out wide.

3. It's time to squeeze some peas! Scrunch up your toes. Pull them in really tight and imagine that you are squeezing and squishing peas with them.

4. Squeeze those peas tight for three seconds . . . and then release your toes. Ahhh.

5. Now tense and squeeze the muscles in your legs and bottom for three seconds, and then relax your muscles. Imagine you are lying on hundreds of peas and you are squishing them underneath your body.

6. Now it's time for your hands. Squeeze your hands into fists and tense the muscles in your arms and your sides and your belly for a count of three. Imagine you are squishing whole bowls full of peas. Hold for three seconds, and then relax.

7. Squeeze up your face. Close your eyes and shut them really tight. See how many peas you can squish with your eyes! Hold for three seconds, and then relax your whole face.

8. Finish with a big, deep belly breath in . . . and then relax your whole body. Well done. You have squished MILLIONS OF PEAS!

10. Bad-dream Buddy

CALMING EXERCISE #1

Having a stuffed buddy with you while you sleep will help you to not feel alone. Sometimes having a bad dream can make you not want to go to bed because you feel scared. But don't be scared—your bad-dream buddy is here.

1. Who would you like to be your bad-dream buddy? Pick one out of all your stuffed toys and teddy bears before you get into bed.

2. Jump into bed with your bad-dream buddy and lie down in a comfortable position.

3. This buddy has magical powers. Don't tell everyone about your buddy—only tell people you love and trust so you can keep it your secret. Your bad-dream buddy can protect you from bad dreams. Your buddy does this by staying with you while you sleep. They dream with you while you dream. They are like your new best friend, who always takes care of you, no matter what.

4. To activate your buddy's magical powers of protection, say, "Bad-dream buddy, keep all the bad dreams away. Sweet dreams only, please."

5. You can say this to your buddy as many times as you wish.

6. Make sure to say this every night to activate your friend's magic. Sweet dreams!

11. Shake It Off

MOOD-CHANGING EXERCISE #3

Do you know the feeling of being really upset or angry or frustrated about something? It can feel so uncomfortable to be in your body during those times. Shaking out the yucky feelings can help you release discomfort. It can make you feel happy and light once again, and that's exactly what you need before bed so you can comfortably fall asleep.

1. Stand up in your bedroom.

2. Music is always a great mood changer, so if there are some lighthearted songs that you like, play one while you do this exercise.

3. Examples that I like include "Shake It Off" by Taylor Swift, "Happy" by Pharrell Williams, and "Can't Stop the Feeling!" by Justin Timberlake. These might help get you off to a good start.

4. Start to jump and shake around. Shake your arms and your legs. Shake off all the yucky feelings from your fingers, your toes, and your head.

5. You can ask your parent or caregiver to jump and shake with you if you want. Trust me—this makes it even more fun.

6. Before long, you will both be laughing and feeling so much better.

7. You will also start to feel like all the yucky feelings have left your body. Are you full of good feelings now? You will know because the good feelings will make you feel happy.

8. If you don't feel better yet, then you may need to do more shaking. If you do feel better, it is time to fall asleep . . . in a much happier mood.

12. Lovebug Meditation

HEART-OPENING EXERCISE

This exercise is going to make you feel very relaxed and will fill up every part of you with love.

1. Lie on your back in bed or sit up with your legs crossed and your back nice and straight.

2. Close your eyes and take a big, slow, deep breath in . . . and then slowly let that breath out.

3. Imagine the color pink in your mind. You will see pink in the space in front of your eyes, even when they are closed.

4. Now focus on your heart and the center of your chest. Imagine that the color pink is covering your heart, like a big blanket wrapping around it.

5. Keep taking nice slow, deep breaths. Every time you breathe in, imagine that the color pink is getting bigger. It spreads across your chest and your shoulders, and then down into your arms and into your hands and your fingers.

6. In your mind, see the color spreading down into your tummy, and then down into your legs and into your feet and your toes.

7. Now it's in your face, your head. Imagine your whole body is now pink. Pink is a loving color—it makes you feel full of love. You are a sweet and compassionate person. You have lots of love to give, and you are loved by a lot of people. This feeling is very nice.

8. Stay still with your eyes closed for as long as you need to in order to feel this feeling. Then fall asleep feeling full of love, just like a lovebug!

13. Light as a Feather

RELAXATION MEDITATION #1

This relaxation meditation will have you feeling light as a feather and floating with the clouds in no time.

1. Lie down in a comfortable position.

2. Close your eyes and shake out all the wiggles to make sure you are super comfy.

3. Wiggle your toes and notice how your feet feel. Using your inner voice, talk to your feet, and tell them to relax. After you do this, you can feel your feet starting to tingle and feel light.

4. Focus on your ankles and lower legs. Tell your feet, ankles, and lower legs to soften down into your bed. Notice them starting to tingle and feel light as well.

5. Now focus on your upper legs. Your legs are so light, and they are feeling very comfortable. Move up to your hips and lower back. Tell them to melt into your bed and let go.

6. Focus on your tummy and become aware of your chest. Imagine that your body is feeling sleepy and as light as a feather. You could float up and away into the sky if you wanted to.

7. Let your arms feel like they are floating as they get tingly and light, too.

8. Allow your entire body to rest. Your whole body feels weightless right now. You could easily drift off to sleep, floating like a feather blowing around in a gentle wind.

14. Dear Diary

DAILY REFLECTION MEDITATION

It is always a good idea to empty all the thoughts out of your head before you go to sleep. Writing in your diary every night will create space in your mind for deep relaxation and sweet dreams. It is good to look back at your day, to notice the ups and downs and how you felt at different times. It is also a great practice to get into the habit of doing this every evening so you can empty all the thoughts out of your head. This will help you fall asleep quickly and easily.

1. Sit up comfortably in your bed.

2. You can use a diary or a journal, or just speak out loud when you ask yourself these questions every night:

   * What made me feel happy today?

   * What made me feel angry today?

   * If I could, what would I change about today to make it better?

   * What do I need to do tomorrow that I didn't get to finish today?

3. Write something kind about yourself right now. You could just write a nice word, or write a whole sweet compliment.

4. Now give yourself a nice big squeeze for being good to yourself. Please, go ahead!

5. If you want to, you can even draw a picture that represents your day. A picture diary would be cool!

6. You can also ask your parent or caregiver to write down for you how you feel, if you wish.

7. Try to repeat this reflection meditation every evening before bed.

8. Now relax . . . and sleep.

15. Silent Ladybug Challenge

SEATED MEDITATION

They say that the number of spots a ladybug has tells how old it is. And if a ladybug is two years old, it can sit quietly and meditate for only two minutes. How many spots do you have? If you are six years old, then you have six spots. Your challenge is to sit quietly in meditation for six minutes. This challenge is not easy. Practice, and you will get better. It is important to be patient—try not to get upset or annoyed with yourself if it is difficult to sit still and be quiet. Just try to enjoy the silence and be proud of yourself for even trying!

1. Set a timer for the same number of minutes as your age.

2. Sit down on your bed with your legs crossed. Bring your back upright so your spine is nice and straight.

3. Relax your head forward slightly, just a little bit. Soften your jaw and your face.

4. Rest your hands comfortably in your lap or on your knees.

5. Start your timer and close your eyes.

6. Focus on your breath. Try to take nice long meditation breaths the whole time you are sitting quietly.

7. Don't worry about your thoughts. It is okay to think during silent meditation. Just imagine that your thoughts are like waves in the ocean: Let them come . . . and let them go.

8. When the timer goes off, you are finished with your meditation. Rest well!

16. wake up, Chakra

CHAKRA AWARENESS MEDITATION

This meditation will help you wake up your seven main chakras so you can feel happy, healthy, and full of good energy.

1. Lie on your back or sit up straight with your legs crossed.

2. The first chakra is at the bottom of your spine. This chakra is red. Close your eyes and imagine the color red at the bottom of your spine. Reach around and gently tap on your first chakra as you say, "Wake up, chakra. Wake up."

3. The second chakra is just below your belly button. This chakra is orange. Close your eyes and imagine the color orange below your belly button. Gently tap on your second chakra as you say, "Wake up, chakra. Wake up."

4. Your third chakra is just above your belly button. This chakra is yellow. Close your eyes and imagine the color yellow right above your belly button. Tap on your third chakra as you say, "Wake up, chakra. Wake up."

5. The fourth chakra is in the middle of your chest, right next to your heart. This chakra is green. Close your eyes and imagine the color green in your chest. Tap on your fourth chakra as you say, "Wake up, chakra. Wake up."

6. The fifth chakra is in your throat. This chakra is blue. Close your eyes and imagine the color blue on your throat. Tap on your fifth chakra as you say, "Wake up, chakra. Wake up."

7. The sixth chakra is in the middle of your forehead. This chakra is indigo (a kind of deep blue in between violet and sky blue). Close your eyes and imagine the color indigo on your forehead. Tap on your sixth chakra as you say, "Wake up, chakra. Wake up."

8. The seventh chakra is found on the top of your head. This chakra is violet. Close your eyes and imagine the color violet on the top of your head. Tap on your seventh chakra as you say, "Wake up, chakra. Wake up." Now that you feel really good, it's time for you to have a great sleep.

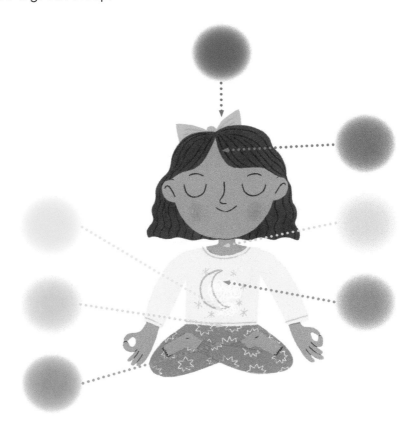

17. What I Like About You

Seeds need water and sunlight to grow. You need water and sunlight, too. You also need love, safety, and the reassurance that you are wonderful. That gives you a good feeling that you are on strong, solid ground. This game is a cute way to find out all the things you like about yourself before you go to sleep. It will help root you to the ground, just like seeds. This will also give you a chance to tell your parent or caregiver what you like about them!

1. Tuck yourself into bed and get cozy. It's time to play the What I Like About You game.

2. Your parent or caregiver can go first, to get the game going.

3. Make sure they tell you something they like about you. It could be something silly or something serious. It can be about your personality, or something physical.

4. You might be happily surprised by what you hear!

5. Now it is your turn. Tell your parent something you like about them.

6. They might be happily surprised by what they hear!

7. Take turns back and forth until you feel like you are happily reassured that you are an awesome being and that your parent or caregiver loves you very much.

8. Say good night to your parent or caregiver in your own special way . . . and then fall happily asleep!

18. My Magical Mind

INTENTION-SETTING EXERCISE

You have a very powerful mind. Your thoughts have a magical energy that can change the way you feel. If you wake up in the morning and think happy, positive thoughts, this might help you have a good day. Do this exercise so you can have a great day tomorrow!

1. Lie in your favorite comfortable position in bed.

2. Take three nice big breaths, in and out. Imagine you are breathing IN relaxation and breathing OUT all your worries.

3. Close your eyes and start to think about tomorrow. What would you like your day to look like?

4. Picture in your mind all the different things you will be doing tomorrow. Start with getting dressed, then going to school, and so on.

5. Now picture everything that you will do tomorrow going well. Picture yourself feeling happy and having a good time with everything you do.

6. When you imagine yourself happy throughout your day tomorrow, see if you can feel that happiness in your body right now. It might feel like butterflies in your tummy, or it might feel like your heart gets bigger in your chest, like the Grinch in the Dr. Seuss book. Smile! When you smile, you send signals through your body that you are happy.

7. All these feelings are making magic inside you. Your magical mind is helping create a good day for you tomorrow, even before it begins.

8. See if you can fall asleep thinking positive thoughts about what tomorrow will bring.

19. Hot Dragon Breath, Cold Penguin Breath

CALMING EXERCISE #2

This exercise is a seated cat-cow yoga asana. If you are not familiar with yoga, you can ask your parent or caregiver to show you what that is. It might be fun for you and your parent to practice this breathing exercise together!

1. Sit up straight in bed.

2. Cross your legs and take ahold of your knees with your hands.

3. When you breathe in, bend forward to round your back. Pull your tummy in toward your spine as you hold on to your knees for support.

4. Make a small O with your lips and breathe in as if you are sucking in through a straw. It should feel like a cool breeze blowing into your mouth. This awesome penguin breathing will cool you down, as if you are breathing icy Arctic air into your body.

5. When you breathe out, arch your back backward and stick out your tummy, still holding on to your knees for support. Breathe out as if you are breathing out fire, like a dragon.

6. Then open your mouth as wide as you can and roar out loud, like a dragon would roar. This hot dragon breath will create heat in your body and cleanse your energy.

7. Repeat breathing in a cool penguin breath and breathing out a hot dragon breath at least 10 times.

8. Don't forget to round your back and pull your belly in as you breathe in, and arch your back, pushing your belly out as you breathe out. Then relax . . . and sleep.

20. Special Shower

PHYSICAL AND VISUAL EXERCISE

This is a fun exercise you can do in the shower before you go to bed.

1. Hop into the shower.

2. You're going to wash like normal but imagine that this shower has special powers. This shower can cleanse you on the outside—and also on the inside.

3. Close your eyes and imagine that this special shower is washing off EVERYTHING that might be making you not feel your best. While the shower can wash away dirt and clean your skin, it can also wash away sadness, anger, loneliness, and fear.

4. Start with your head. Wash your hair and imagine that you are washing away any bad thoughts as well. Imagine that the shower is washing your brain and making it shiny-clean so it is full of only good, happy thoughts.

5. Wash your body and imagine that the special shower is taking away all your tiredness. It is filling your body with good feelings and good energy so you will feel all new and clean before bed.

6. When you look down, imagine that all the yuck you're washing off is being taken away, down the drain.

7. From the top of your head to the tips of your toes, inside and out, you now feel squeaky-clean.

8. Now put on your comfy PJs and snuggle into bed. Sweet, sparkling dreams!

21. Belly Breathing

Deep breathing is very good for all of us. It helps us relax our body and mind so we can fall asleep easily. You can also do this type of breathing if you are feeling stressed or upset about something and you would like to calm yourself down.

1. Lie on your back like a starfish, with your arms and legs comfortably out to your sides.

2. Close your eyes.

3. Take a nice deep breath. Breathe all the way down into your tummy. Make sure your tummy fills up like a big balloon.

4. Hold your breath there for one or two seconds, and then breathe all the way out until your tummy is completely empty.

5. Breathe in again and see if you can fill your tummy even more this time. Make your belly feel even more like a full balloon.

6. Hold your breath there for one or two seconds, and then breathe all the way out until your tummy is completely empty.

7. Repeat this belly-breathing exercise 10 times. You should feel very calm and relaxed when you are finished.

8. If you feel like you need to, repeat your big belly breaths as many times as it takes for you to get relaxed enough to fall asleep easily.

22. Bubble Mansion

RELAXATION MEDITATION #2

This meditation will help you imagine that you are in another world far, far away, a place where you feel very floaty and relaxed.

1. Make sure you are comfortably tucked in your bed.

2. Close your eyes and reach into your imagination.

3. Imagine you just blew the biggest bubble you have ever blown before. It is even big enough for you to climb inside it!

4. All of a sudden, this giant bubble starts to rise off the ground. It floats up toward the clouds, and then it goes right into a cloud. Inside the cloud you see an enormous mansion that looks like it was made from one big bubble. It's a bubble mansion in the sky!

5. A big pink bubble floats over to you and says, "Welcome to Bubble Mansion. We have been expecting you. Are you having trouble sleeping? Follow me! I have just the thing to help you sleep."

6. Now what you see in front of you is the bounciest, softest, comfiest bubble bed you could ever imagine. The pink bubble says, "Go over to the bed, and lie down on it and close your eyes."

7. You do this, and instantly you start to dream. You dream about being in a giant bubble that floats up into a cloud, where there is a hidden bubble mansion waiting for you with the comfiest bed in the world.

8. Imagine your bed is the comfiest bubble bed in the world, making you feel floaty and very, very relaxed. . . .

23. Brave in the Dark

IMAGINATION GAME #1

Are you sometimes afraid of the dark? Do you sometimes wish you had a friend there with you? Have fun playing with your imagination and your favorite animal in this bedtime game that's designed to help you feel safe when the lights are out.

1. Lie down comfortably in bed. Close your eyes for a few seconds and notice that everything is dark behind your eyes. Now open your eyes.

2. Your challenge is to pretend that the darkness you see when you close your eyes is a big chalkboard that you can draw on. You imagine a bowl of chalk on the ground. You will use the chalk in a moment.

3. What is your favorite animal? Once you decide, close your eyes again.

4. Choose a piece of chalk from the bowl—whichever color you want to use.

5. Draw your favorite animal on the chalkboard there in front of you. Have fun drawing your animal.

6. Now watch as your favorite animal comes to life on the chalk-board. This new friend is very happy to see you!

7. You can talk to your animal in your mind. Tell your animal to turn around in circles or sit down on the ground. This animal is your new best friend. Don't forget to give your new friend a name!

8. You can tell your animal anything, and your friend will keep you company every night. All you have to do is close your eyes to create this magic. The darkness won't be scary anymore, and your new best friend will be right there with you whenever you are going to sleep.

24. Fairy Forest

BREATHING MEDITATION #2

In this breathing meditation, let these sweet little fairies help you breathe nice and slow so you can relax and fall into fairy dreams!

1. Jump into bed and get comfy.

2. Take a nice deep breath in, and when you breathe out, make a gentle sound, like a sigh or a yawn. Do this three times, in and out each time.

3. Close your eyes. Imagine that you are in a forest, where it is very quiet and peaceful. You can hear the birds singing and the wind blowing through the leaves on the trees as you walk through this forest.

4. Up ahead, you see a really big tree. You lie down on the ground under the big tree so you can look up at the sky and watch the leaves blowing in the wind. You feel very relaxed and happy here underneath this big tree.

5. When you look closer at the leaves, you notice something very magical. You see fairies! There are lots and lots of very tiny fairies.

6. Two happy fairies come down to you to say hello. They both sit on your tummy and smile at you. They giggle when your tummy moves up and down as you breathe. It's like a roller coaster ride. You have to take deep breaths in and out so the fairies can have a fun ride on your roller coaster tummy.

7. Soon the fairies get tired, so they lie down on your tummy to sleep. You slow down your breathing so they can stay still and quiet.

8. You are tired, too. You feel very safe and happy, and so comfortable and sleepy. Happy snoozing!

25. Feel Better

VISUALIZATION MEDITATION #1

It's never great when you're sick and not feeling your best. Allow this sweet visualization meditation to transport you to another world, where the cupcake cuties will take good care of you!

1. Lie down in your favorite position on your bed.

2. Make sure you have a snuggly blanket and a soft stuffed animal, and that you are wearing your comfiest pajamas.

3. Close your eyes and use your imagination.

4. Imagine you are in a magical elevator. You press a button, and the elevator stops and the doors open. You step out and look down . . . and you find yourself standing on green grass. But this grass is different—it feels soft and squishy underneath your feet. It turns out that the grass is made of frosting! You could eat it if you wanted to. Now you see that *everything* in this magical place is something you can eat. The clouds in the sky are made of marshmallows. The trees are licorice sticks—all different flavors. The path is made from cookie crumbs, and the lake is one big strawberry shake.

5. You learn that the people who live here are called cupcake cuties. They are little people who look just like cupcakes. They tell you about a special tree that can make you feel better when you touch it.

6. You walk over to the tree and put your hands on its trunk. You can feel a gentle tingling sensation in your hands.

7. The tingles travel up your arms and all over your body, making you feel so much better.

8. The cupcake cuties bring cheer because they are so happy for you. They're ready for you to taste the clouds and drink from the strawberry shake lake with them. Sweet dreams!

26. Get Rid of the Wiggles

INTERACTIVE EXERCISE

This fun exercise is designed to help you release your extra energy and put you in a calm, lighthearted, happy mood before bed.

1. Make sure you are tucked in bed and ready to do some exercises to get all the wiggles out of you.

2. First, giggle out the wiggles by making a funny face. Be sure it's the craziest, funniest face you've ever made.

3. Next, roll out the wiggles by rolling from one side of your bed to the other, back and forth five times. If you want to go fast, go fast!

4. Then shimmy out the wiggles by shimmying like a snake in your bed. Shimmy your whole body five times.

5. Pop out the wiggles by popping like popcorn, up and down for five seconds. Do this three times.

6. Yawn out your wiggles by pretending to yawn five times. (This might make you yawn for real!)

7. Finally, breathe out your wiggles by taking five long, slow, deep breaths in . . . and out.

8. Now lie still, like a statue, and allow your body to rest there so you can fall asleep . . . wiggle-free.

27. Moon and Stars

BREATHING MEDITATION #3

This simple exercise combines counting and breathing. If you follow the steps, you will be sleepy and relaxed in no time!

1. Lie down in a comfortable position.

2. Close your eyes for a few seconds and notice that everything looks black behind your eyes.

3. In this breathing meditation, imagine that the blackness is the night sky.

4. Keeping your eyes closed, imagine that on the left there are 20 stars all gathered together. On the right, you see a big full moon. The stars want to be with the moon, but for them to get there, you will have to take a deep breath.

5. When you take one deep breath, one star will fly up and over to the moon. You have to take 20 deep breaths to help all 20 stars fly over to the moon.

6. Ready? Close your eyes and see the 20 stars on the left and the big full moon on the right. Breathe in . . . and watch one star fly up and over to the moon.

7. Then breathe out and relax. Make sure to count the stars to keep track of them each time you breathe in to let one join the moon. Think you've got it? The whole idea is to relax. You might lose count, or you might get so sleepy that you just end up falling asleep. Or you might need to start all over again if you're still not tired at the end of your 20 breaths. It's okay.

8. Close your eyes and start breathing. Help all those stars get to the moon. . . .

28. Roar Like a Lion

FUN BREATHING EXERCISE

With this exercise, you can pretend to be several animals! Each animal will help you exercise different muscles in your face as you breathe in different ways.

1. Make sure you are tucked in bed and ready to do some fun animal impressions.

2. Lion's breath: Take in a deep breath, and then open your mouth really wide and roar like a lion.

3. As you roar, breathe out all your breath. Do this three times.

4. Cow's breath: Take in a big, deep breath, then push your lips forward and moo like a cow.

5. As you moo, breathe out all your breath. Do this three times.

6. Dog's breath: Stick out your tongue and take in short, fast breaths, in and out, panting like a dog.

7. Pant for ten seconds. Do this three times.

8. Horse's breath: Take in a big, deep breath and make a *neigh* sound. As you breathe out, relax and shake your face and head, neighing loudly like a horse for as long as you can. Do this three times. Now . . . sleep.

29. The What-If Game

In this game, you can use your imagination to create funny, yummy, crazy things. Do you think you can beat me? Okay! Are you ready?

1. What if when you tickled people too much, it made them explode? That would be so funny! Your turn! What if . . .

2. What if your bed was made of your favorite candy and you could snack on it all night long? What is your favorite candy? Your turn! What if . . .

3. What if your shoes were magical and you could jump as high as the tallest trees? That would be super cool! Your turn! What if . . .

4. What if your pet could talk to you? A magical dog or cat would be awesome, right? Your turn! What if . . .

5. What if you could chew on bubble gum, then blow a bubble so big, you started to float off the ground and up into the sky? Would you visit the sun or the moon? Your turn! What if . . .

6. Now close your eyes. Imagine your big giant bubble gum bubble that you have just blown is lifting you up off your bed. You are floating like a balloon into the sky.

7. You are getting lighter and lighter. It feels really relaxing to float around in the sky like a big bubble. You feel as free as a bird flying up above the trees and the houses.

8. Let yourself float off into sweet dreams. . . .

30. White Light

This is a nice visualization meditation you can use to feel peaceful before sleep. You can also use your mind to help make your friends feel as good as you do!

1. Lie down comfortably in bed or sit up straight with your legs crossed, your hands resting in your lap.

2. Close your eyes and take a nice big, deep breath.

3. Imagine in your mind that you are sitting in a circle with your friends. Everyone's eyes are closed, and you are meditating together.

4. There is a ball of white light floating above all your heads. The light is slowly moving in circles above your group, around and around.

5. Using the power of your mind, you can stop the light at any time. You can make the light stop over anyone in the circle, including yourself.

6. Whenever the light stops, it shines down onto the person below, filling them with loving energy. The light makes them feel happy, loved, and very peaceful.

7. Make the white light move around the circle so it stops over every person, taking turns to fill everyone up with happiness, love, and peace.

8. Don't forget to fill yourself up with this magical white light so you can feel wonderful before you fall asleep!

Where to Learn More About Meditation

Here are some resources where you can find more information about meditation. Some will connect you to me out in the world, and some will show you other great resources I really like.

YouTube Channels

Corys ConsciousLiving: Children's bedtime stories and meditations (https://www.youtube.com/channel/UCfD6_TOQXwPmamZdOnEN8sg)

This is my YouTube channel, a place where you can find hundreds of meditation stories I have created to help children learn to meditate, fall asleep, and deal with daily problems. You might need an adult to show you how to find my channel, but once you are there, you can find the stories all by yourself!

New Horizon: Meditation and sleep stories (https://www.youtube.com/user/NewHorizonHolistic)

On this wonderful channel, you'll find guided meditations, sleep stories, bedtime stories, and kids' meditations. Once you have the help of an adult to get started, you'll be able to visit this channel safely on your own.

APPS

InsightTimer: Adults' and children's meditations (https://insighttimer.com)

This app allows you to listen and learn to meditate with me, and with many other meditation teachers. An adult might need to help you find the right teacher for you and show you how the app works, but then you'll find it's easy and you can use it on your own.

Headspace for Kids: Meditation for kids (https://www.headspace.com/meditation/kids)

Children and their caregivers can enjoy fun, engaging activities that teach them the basics of mindfulness. This website is available to all subscribers, and you will need an adult to help you get started. You can practice breathing exercises, visualization, focusing, and more.

BOOKS

My children's books at ajnahypnotherapy.com: *Charlie the Lost Penguin* and *Claire Gets Stuck in the Mud!*

I wrote these books with awesome messages for kids just like you! Claire is a pig who gets stuck in the mud. She meets lots of friends who help her out. And Charlie is a penguin who doesn't know where he belongs. He meets friends who help him find his home. Check them out!

My children's book on Amazon: *Sarah's Rainbow Angel (Create Space, 2000)*

I wrote this book to help children learn that they are very powerful and strong and can make themselves feel better when they are hurt.

I Am a Warrior Goddess by Jennifer Adams (Sounds True, 2018)

I like this book, and I think you will, too. It has a good message about how each day you have opportunities to make a positive impact with ordinary actions. We all want to be good people, and this book has lots of great examples for how we can do that.

Meditate with Me: A Step-by-Step Mindfulness Journey by Mariam Gates (Dial Books, 2017)

This gentle, clear book is a pleasure to use. You will learn how to focus on your breath, be aware of the sensations in your body, and settle your busy mind.

Podcasts

The Corys ConsciousLiving podcast: Children's meditation stories. This is on Google Play and iTunes, as well as on Podbean: https://corysconscious living.podbean.com.

My podcast channel is another place to listen to my meditation stories. You can also ask an adult to help you download my stories from there so you can listen to them without having to be on the Internet. Once you are shown how to work the podcast, I am sure you can do it all by yourself.

Acknowledgments

I would like to acknowledge my children, Jenna and Isabelle. Thank you for all the lessons of life and love you have shown me over the years. You two beautiful souls don't let me get away with anything but being my best self in this life. I am forever grateful for you both choosing me to be your momma on this journey!

About the Author

Cory Cochiolo, MA, CHt, has been a certified hypnotherapist since 2004 and a certified hypnotherapy teacher since 2008. She has a master's degree in transpersonal psychology from the International University of Professional Studies. Cory has her own private practice in San Diego, California, where she works with clients on a daily basis. She also specializes in teaching meditation classes in her community.

Cory has a successful YouTube channel, Corys ConsciousLiving, which focuses on both adult's and children's meditations and has had over 9 million views to date. Her latest endeavor is podcasting!

Through her various business ventures, Cory is dedicated to using her knowledge to help people. She is also the author of many children's books, including Sarah's Rainbow Angel, a book that teaches children from a very early age how to heal themselves with sound and color.

CPSIA information can be obtained
at www.ICGtesting.com
Printed in the USA
JSHW041040230720
6788JS00004BB/7

9 781646 114542